An Island Nurse

Sheila Chapman

authorHOUSE®

AuthorHouse™ UK Ltd.
500 Avebury Boulevard
Central Milton Keynes, MK9 2BE
www.authorhouse.co.uk
Phone: 08001974150

First published by AuthorHouse 4/6/2009

ISBN: 978-1-4389-3543-0 (sc)

Printed in the United States of America
Bloomington, Indiana

This book is printed on acid-free paper.

Contents

Foreword

Chapter 1
The Early Years   5

Chapter 2
The Nurse's Training   25

Chapter 3
Getting Married   47

Chapter 4
Sailing Home   57

Chapter 5
No Sense of Direction   65

Chapter 6
Leaving Stroma   77

Foreword

This book is the 80-year long memory of an innocent young girl, brought up in a village community unaware of the harsher and broader issues in life. A journey through good times and sad, together amounting to a good and prosperous life, which sadly came to an end recently.

Elizabeth Laird Manson died after a short illness on 8th August 2007 therefore this book is dedicated to her.

This book is a tribute to our Mam who brought us up to respect things in life and to value what we have. As she used to say to us all when we were younger, "Money doesn't buy happiness" and "Life is what *you* make it". Truer words were never spoken, for she gave us a sure footing on the road to life and for this we will always be grateful.

We will always treasure the love that she gave us, and be grateful for the encouragement to "make something of ourselves". We were never pressured into being something we were not; we did our best as she did for us.

She was certainly a mother above all Mothers, and we love and miss her very much.

Chapter 1

The Early Years

John O' Groats villa (circa 1920's)

Elizabeth Laird Manson was born on the 27th of November 1926 in a well-known Northern Scottish village called John o' Groats (locally known as Groats) at the very North tip of mainland Scotland. Little did anyone know when she was born that she was destined to be the district nurse on the Island of Stroma. The island of Stroma lies between John o' Groats and the Islands of Orkney, a few miles from her home, and from where her story begins.

Elizabeth, affectionately known as 'Bessie', grew up in Groats in the late 1920's. Her father was the local postmaster who owned the local Post Office and Shop. Bessie's mother worked in the Post Office and shop whilst bringing up her family. Bessie was the third youngest of a family of six, two boys and four girls and lived in a house called John O' Groats Villa, a two storey house was home to her family.

She attended the John o' Groats primary school that hosted around fifty local children and had two teachers. The school itself had two rooms, the little room, which was used for the primary children and held five classes, and the big room where the children were taught secondary education. In the big room set in the middle, stood a high round stove, a bit like an old-fashioned letterbox. The stove had to be stoked by the teacher who had to lift the heavy round lid on top to put coal into it. A rail completely surrounded the stove to stop the children touching the hot surface.

As this was the only heating in the school it needed fuel put on regularly to keep the fire going. As most of the children walked to school in all weathers, they would sometimes get soaked with rain and have to hang their coats in the cloakroom to dry.

The teacher would then get all the children to stand around the rail and flap their arms to get themselves warm before sitting down to their lessons at their desks. School started at 9.30am and the children got out again at 1pm for lunch. Bessie and her sister would run the short distance home at lunchtime for their lunch and then return to school for 2pm. School would then finished at 4pm and the children would run home to put on their old clothes so they could go out to play with their friends.

Bessie loved school and got on well with her friends; she was a very sociable child and was never lost for anything to say. Like all children in those days, fashion was not an option unlike nowadays, but there were times when they liked to dress up when going out.

Bessie's hair was as straight as a die and, when she was going to a party or any event, her mother would put tin curlers in her and her sister Isobel's hair to make it a bit curlier, and give it a bit of a frizz. Tin curlers were pieces of aluminium, two or three inches by half an inch, bent over in two, with a bit which bent over and slipped up when in the hair to hold it in place. Bessie's mother also had curling tongs, which she set in the fire, and curled their hair with the heat. You had to be experienced in the use of these, because if they were too hot they would singe your hair.

Bessie and Isobel thought this was great, and it made them feel grown up as they showed off their new hairstyle to their friends. One day when Bessie went to school she could hardly concentrate on her lessons, as one of the local girls who had the most beautiful dark thick hair had decided to try putting tin curlers in her hair too. Bessie's laughter was irrepressible as she looked at the girl's hair, which reminded her of the brush her father used to use to clean the chimney. The girl's hair stood out like the chimney brush all around her head, and the more Bessie tried not to laugh the more hysterical she got.

The teacher had even lost patience with Bessie and told her to leave her desk and stand with her back to the class until she pulled herself together. However this made no difference, since all the children could still see were Bessie's shoulders going up and down as she laughed inwardly. Even when Bessie tried to compose herself the image of the girl's hair would wander back into her mind and once again would set her off laughing.

Eventually, since the teacher could not get anything remotely comprehensible from Bessie's mouth she sent her home. After school the teacher then visited and asked Bessie's mother if she could explain what was wrong with her. Her mother answered that she couldn't get any sense out of her at all, as each time she asked her what had happened Bessie would burst into whoops of laughter once again, and she thought it better to leave her until she calmed down.

Bessie laughed for about two days solid, still unable to share her hysteria with anyone as she felt so bad for laughing at this poor young girl. Thankfully the fact that Bessie had been unable to tell anyone had saved the girl from embarrassment because she did not know what Bessie had found so funny either.

Part of the curriculum at school was sewing which was to help prepare the girls when embarking on their own dressmaking and providing themselves with skills to help achieve this. The children would lift the desk lid and keep their sewing in their desks. This practice was easier for them because they could lay their threads and material in it, which was simpler than working on a sloping desk.

This particular day it was a small class of five pupils because the rest of them were off school with the flu. Bessie was finishing off a square that she had tirelessly worked on, and was very proud of her effort. She was just finishing off the last side when she happened to look up only to see another girl peeping round the side of her desk wearing her Grannie's little tin spectacles on the point of her nose. As usual Bessie started to laugh but, as she laughed, she accidentally spat on her lovely square cloth. This only fuelled her laughter even more, as she looked down at the sodden piece of material. Bessie launched herself into the body of her desk so the teacher would not hear her cries of hysteria as she tried to pull herself together.

After composing herself long enough to calm down she started to gather her square of sewing once again looked up. Once more to her dismay, the same girl was peeping around the opposite side of the desk with the spectacles still sitting on the point of her nose. Bessie was doubled up with laughter by this time, and unable to come out from behind the desk. All she could do was sit there until the end of class, when desk lids were put back down. Thankfully for Bessie, this time, the teacher was unaware of anything untoward going on as all desk lids were up, blocking her view of the pupils.

Eventually the school was reduced to one teacher because the pupil numbers had decreased. Bessie's teacher was a Mrs Manson from Stroma, and she had taught Bessie all through primary school until she was old enough to go to the High School. Once the children reached 11 years of age they attended the Wick High School, an hour's drive away on the school bus.

Mam and Isobel

Bessie loved school; Mental Arithmetic was one of her favourite subjects, English also. She did very well in the writing competitions, winning the overall competition in her class one year, writing about the prevention of cruelty to animals.

Bessie tried to do well at school, and then went on to Wick High School with her mind set on becoming a nurse. She was planning to go to school until she was sixteen, sit her exams, then go away to do her sick children's nurses training, her general nurse training and then maternity nurses training.
Bessie wanted to be a nurse so much that she would skip one afternoon of High School each week to go down to the local maternity hospital, the Henderson Home, where her older sister Mary worked.

Here she spent her time in the baby nursery, helping getting the baby bottles ready, making their beds and folding up the clean laundry. However she was only allowed to hold the babies, otherwise her sister would get into trouble. Bessie was quite content with this as, to her, it was sheer heaven, and only reinforced that her goal in life was to be a nurse. Her mother, completely oblivious to these truancies, assumed her daughter was at school. Bessie did nothing to alleviate her assumption and her sister never mentioned it either. As usual the two sisters set off on their journey to school by bus, went to the High School and then returned home at night the same way.

One particular day, as the sisters returned home from school, Bessie and her younger sister Isobel were surprised when the minister stopped the bus about a mile from Groats and told the driver that she and her sister would be getting off there and staying with them for a while. Bessie was beside herself with worry, and couldn't understand why on earth they would be staying at the minister's house, but in those days you were told nothing and you certainly didn't question the minister.

After what seemed an eternity the girls had finished their dinner when the minister's wife explained to them that there had been a fire at their house, and it was completely destroyed. The fire had started upstairs and had spread through the house. The family tried desperately to save what they had in the house however Bessie's father told them to leave it, as their own life was more important. It took so long for the fire engine to arrive there was nothing left to save and unfortunately there was a problem with the insurance and it ended up that the house was not covered at the time of the fire.

The minister's wife told the girls that they weren't to worry as everyone was okay, and Bessie and Isobel were to stay with them overnight. Bessie worried even more, and went up to the attic bedroom with her sister to go to bed. She was upset enough about the fact that there had been a fire in their home, but when the minister's wife handed them a candle and sent them off to bed they were even more frightened of the burning candle.

They both peered out of the skylight and looked towards Groats, to see a cloud of black smoke which they assumed could only be the remains of their home. Too scared to get undressed for bed they snuggled up together, made sure the candle was out, and waited for the next morning to arrive. As the sun rose the next morning Bessie thought about her mother and father and wondered what the house looked like and whether they would have saved anything? What about their clothes, had they saved anything?

The two girls were sent on their way to school on the bus as usual, but they couldn't understand why they had not been able to see their mother and father. They were told nothing which only added to their anxiety and wondered when they would be allowed home. The day at school was long and tiresome for the two girls who had hardly slept the night before and eventually came to an end.

In the John O Groat Journal 1940, that week it wrote, "a large John O' Groats dwelling-house belonging to Mr Hugh Manson, merchant, was left completely gutted, with only the walls left standing after a fire swept through it. The blaze started when the chimney caught alight and quickly spread through the upper storey of the house after one of the rafters ignited. Mr Manson and several neighbours were immediately on the scene and made strenuous efforts to quench the outbreak with buckets of water, but their efforts were to no avail".

On returning home from school that night their father met them from the bus, and they were taken to their new temporary home. There was a house adjoining the Post Office which belonged to a local resident. He allowed them to live in the one end for the time being, until they could sort out a permanent residence. Bessie didn't care where they stayed, as long as they were all together. Bessie's mother and father slept in the main room with Bessie's youngest sister. Isobel and Bessie slept on a bed which had a rubber ground sheet under it to stop the rain soaking through it, where buckets were strategically placed to catch raindrops, as the roof leaked. Whilst this was adequate for their needs, her brothers were despatched to sleep in the office.

This was to be their home for some time, until Bessie's brother managed to build something more suitable. A kennel which had been built for the dog was later incorporated into a kitchen with an Elsinel, or dry toilet, at the back. It was business as usual, on a temporary basis, until other accommodation was organised. Bessie didn't care what it was like, just that they were all together again and for now life carried on as normal.

As was quite usual illnesses and infections were passed around all the local children, it was inevitable that they avoid them. Bessie and Isobel were at high school one day, in the gym class, when they noticed lots of spots on their bodies. When they came home from school their mother discovered it was, in fact, chickenpox. They had to stay home for two weeks in quarantine, and then another clear week before they could go back to school.

Three weeks was a long time to be at home especially when you felt okay and Bessie was desperate to get back to school to learn, whereas her sister Isobel was quite happy to be at home.
Once quarantine was over Bessie was back to school like a shot to see what she had missed. Bessie worked hard at her subjects and loved her time there. However when Bessie was just fifteen and a half her father became ill.

He had been in hospital for four weeks with a very large stone in his bladder and had been very poorly. He began to feel a lot better and had come home for one night, but his health deteriorated greatly which resulted in him having to be put back into hospital where he died shortly after. The medical profession was not as advanced in those days as they are nowadays. Bessie's father must have known he was very poorly, because he had asked her if she would help her mother run the post office and shop, and look after her youngest sister. Of course Bessie agreed to her father's request. She was only a child herself and had not expected him to die, and thought by reassuring him would make him feel better at the time.

His death was not just a devastating blow because Bessie was so young, but she had promised her father before he died to fulfil his request and she had to abide by it. Bessie had no inclination to work in a shop of any description, because she wanted to be a nurse. However, in those days respect for her mother's situation, and the loss of her father, overrode any preference to be a nurse for the moment. Her mother and family needed her help and support so she left the school, and there ended her dream of a nursing career.

Bessie became accustomed to the way her life was to go towards and just had to accept and get on with it. She told herself to count her blessings as she still had her mother and siblings and that was a lot more than some poor folk had. Bessie and her younger sister Isobel were still very close and as teenagers got up to quite a bit of mischief.

On one particular occasion their mother asked them to walk up to the east end of Groats to get some milk from their Granny, and a pair of knitting needles she needed. They walked up the road to their Granny's house, which was about a mile away. Bessie's cousin was at her Granny's when they arrived. He had been delivering some things in the East End with his friends in the lorry and had stayed on for some hospitality, and indeed looked quite happy and inebriated. Bessie duly asked for the items requested by her mother and collected them, and she and her sister turned to leave and make their way back down the road.

Her cousin shouted to the two girls as they left to take the lorry down the road with them, if they wanted, to save their feet. Bessie and Isobel didn't need to be told twice, her cousin just lived above the Post Office where his father had a haulage business, and it would save them a good bit of time. Because of her height Bessie couldn't reach the lorry's pedals, so Isobel had to work the pedals and Bessie steered the lorry. The fact that the war was on and there was a blackout didn't faze the two sisters in any way at all as they set off on their journey.

As was typical of Bessie's dare devil attitude, going home with the lorry would have been too easy, so they decided to take the lorry for a run up to Duncansby Head Lighthouse. The lighthouse road is a very windy single-track road indeed, bad enough to drive in daylight but a sight worse in the dark, and especially by two short young girls. However, despite the dangers they faced, Bessie steered the lorry and Isobel worked the clutch, brake and throttle and they eventually arrived back at their uncle's house and parked the lorry up.

The two sisters skipped the short way home and presented their mother with the milk, but when she asked where the knitting pins were they looked at each other and then said that they must have forgotten them. The truth was that one of them had left them lying in the lorry. Unable to go back to retrieve them for fear of getting into trouble, they were soon forgotten.

The next morning Bessie's uncle arrived at the Post Office and after chatting for a while commented on how strange it was that he had found a pair of knitting needles in the lorry. He couldn't understand where they had come from and why they should be in his lorry. He also mentioned the fact that he had never seen his lorry parked in such a way before. Bessie and Isobel said they couldn't understand how the knitting pins had got there either. Later they wondered if their uncle had been impressed with their parking or appalled, neither was sure and it was never mentioned again.

Bessie and her siblings were brought up in a religious household and the family abided by all things holy. Sunday was a day for the Kirk and not for play. It was the Wee Free Kirk first thing, Sunday school in the afternoon and a prayer meeting at night. Every Sunday the family walked the three miles to the church and back home again. Each time Bessie's mother would administer the two sisters with five pandrop sweeties each. This act prevented crackling of other sweetie papers and usually kept them quiet throughout the church service, because in those days children were to be seen and not heard.

When seated in the Kirk pews, as the minister entered the congregation would stand as a mark of respect. Bessie thought this was more to do with straightening her best Sunday coat and making herself presentable than an act of respect. One Sunday, as silence fell and the congregation stood, there was the sound of a ping, ping, ping and ping on the floor. To Bessie's horror all her pandrops had sequentially fallen from a hole in her coat pocket. You could have heard a pandrop! Thank goodness she had eaten one before the service began.

A gentleman standing not far from Bessie, with a curly moustache, turned and grunted "Is this yours?" Once again, as Bessie had so often experienced, a feeling of terrible hysterical tremors began in her chest as she grimaced at the man with her face scarlet. And, if that wasn't bad enough, her sister Isobel was bent double with laughter, and shaking profusely beside her.

Bessie was affronted and even worse was the fact that her sister was still laughing whilst she was trying to pull herself together for fear of getting a terrible telling off from her mother when she got home. Just getting through a service with these girls was a feat in itself.

There was still the Sunday school to go to, which Bessie enjoyed as she loved reading and learning all about Jesus. The Bible was the one thing that they absolutely had to look after. They each had one, and from this they learnt all there was to know about their religion. They were not allowed to play with normal playing cards. Any games on a Sunday had to be played with religious cards, and from this Bessie up until the time she died could recite all the books of the Bible.

One particular story, which Bessie can remember being told at Sunday school, was that of a girl who always took the biggest sweetie when offered any. One day when she ate the sweetie she died, as it had been poisoned. Bessie was not sure why this story had been told to them at Sunday school; however it certainly had a lasting impact on the girls. From then on anytime they were offered a sweetie they always took the smallest ones, for fear of taking the biggest one and being poisoned.

Eventually a bus started commuting the congregation to the church. Bessie can't remember why this happened, perhaps it was because a lot of the congregation were getting older and finding it hard walking the three miles to church each Sunday. However, the bus gave great scope for Bessie and her sister to discuss the various hats that the woman wore to church and there were certainly some discussions that brought on bouts of hysteria too.

Bessie, her sister and the local children used to congregate outside the Post Office. One particular night, just up the road, they were sitting in her Uncles lorry chatting with her friends. Bessie eventually jumped out of the lorry when it was time to go home and wrenched her knee. The pain in Bessie's knee was excruciating causing her to cripple home and explain to her mother what had happened. Bessie's mother thought she had just staved her knee and she was made to lie on the couch for a few days in order to reduce a build up of fluid on her knee.

Bessie although wanting to be a nurse herself was not the best of patients, but had to content herself in order to rest her knee. She was lying on the couch one afternoon when her sister and her friend came in to check on her. The two visitors lit a cigarette and gave it to Bessie. "Hold on", said Bessie "Wait and see if I can aim the fireplace in case Mam comes through". Despite the fact that they knew what they were doing wasn't appropriate for girls their age, the sheer excitement spurred them on. Bessie took the unlit cigarette and tested it out her aim and it worked perfectly. Bessie was feeling quite pleased with herself when Isobel and her friend went off out.

Bessie was lying on the couch having a fly puff on her cigarette when she heard her mother coming through. She took up aim and darted the cigarette towards the fireplace, resulting in it bouncing off the fire rung and landing nicely on the rug, just in front of the fire. Bessie held her breath as her mother went over and picked the offending article up and placed it in the fire. She then walked out saying nothing at all, which only added to Bessie's shame and embarrassment.

As was usual in the Post Office local people would come to the shop with their local produce, it would be bought by Bessie's mother and then sold in the shop, any excess being sent onto the egg market or shops in Wick. One particular day whilst working in the shop, Bessie not the least bit interested in being there, was looking out of the window to see what was happening in the small village. She saw a local woman coming down the road with a big basket which held about twelve dozen eggs, "oh well" she thought at least that'll give me something to do when sorting out all those eggs. People intrigued Bessie and this woman was no exception, she was a tall, big-busted woman who stood tall and straight and had a distinctive laugh.

As Bessie continued to watch out the window she saw the woman take a terrible tumble. She gasped with concern, however once seeing that the woman was unhurt her sympathy didn't last long as she began to feel a terrible tremor inside her as the hysterics overwhelmed her once again.

The woman had managed to get up and gather herself together, and was coming into the Post Office nonetheless Bessie was by this time uncontrollable. As she entered the shop entrance all Bessie could see were egg yolks hanging from her eyelashes. It was at this point that Bessie threw herself under the counter completely helpless. Bessie's outbursts of hysteria were not unknown, and whether it was a nervous disposition she had we will never know, as they have followed her throughout her entire life.

Bessie's mother however was so sympathetic to the woman that this just fuelled Bessie's hysteria. Her mother sat the woman down and went and got a cloth for her to wipe her face clean of eggs. Each time Bessie's mother said "Poor

Nellie." groans were heard coming from behind the counter. Unbeknown to poor Nellie these were, in fact, Bessie's groans of despair which she had to suffer, staying put under the cash drawer until the woman departed from the shop. Seeing the effect that these episodes had on Bessie a realisation must have struck her mother; that her daughter was just not cut out to work in a shop.

Despite the fact that Bessie's mother needed help in the shop she couldn't help but wonder whether her daughter would grow out of these hysterics through time.

In the months that followed it transpired that the postmistress from Huna had to go to Edinburgh for a medical check up, so Bessie was required to help out for one month at the Huna Post Office. Bessie's mother was happy to allow Bessie to go, and she was given two days training beforehand. As she was too young to sign the money order books the postmistress's brother had to oversee all these transactions. Unfortunately for his sister the medical check up discovered something quite serious, and the poor woman died shortly afterwards.

In any event Bessie continued to carry out her Post Office duties at Huna, for two pounds per week, for the following year and a half. It was during this time that she had to be admitted to hospital quite urgently and would experience first hand nursing care.

For a few weeks previously Bessie hadn't been feeling too well, and was having trouble keeping awake. The fact that she had to walk the three miles to her work in the morning, and back at night, did nothing to alleviate this condition. One day she woke up with a terribly sore stomach, but in those days people didn't take days off work they just got on with it, so she walked the three miles to work over snow-covered ground.
One of the Post Office staff's duties at that time was to take down telegrams over the radiophone. The telegram was

being communicated from the island of Stroma, and at the end of each command the speaker would say "Over". This particular telegram had 35 words in it but, as Bessie had fallen asleep during the complete exchange, the only word she was aware of was "Over". She had to ask the person to repeat the message again before recording it correctly. Bessie couldn't understand what was wrong with her she just felt so tired all the time.

The housekeeper at the Huna Post Office was a kindly person who always made a fly cuppa in the morning. As usual Bessie joined the housekeeper and the postmaster in the sitting room, took up her position on the small creepy stool, and drank her cup of tea. The next thing she knew she was lying in a heap on the floor, as she had fallen asleep again and fallen off the stool.

It was worrying for the postmaster as he assumed that Bessie had been burning the candle at both ends, and he told her he was going to speak to her mother about her having such late nights. The fact was that Bessie was unable to do much else other than sleep, so a busy social life was the last thing on her mind.

The housekeeper told Bessie in the afternoon that she thought she should go home as she looked unwell. "I can't," she said, but she was adamant that if Bessie was unwell she would go home. At this point Bessie didn't have the strength to argue with her, or really care, because all that was in her mind was sleep.

The housekeeper went down to the Smiddy where the postmaster, who was also the blacksmith, was working and informed him she was sending Bessie home on the bus because she was unwell. Bessie was despatched on the three o'clock bus to Groats and, as might be expected, fell asleep. The bus driver woke her up in time to get off at her stop.

Hearing what had happened Bessie's mother phoned the doctor who, on examination, confirmed that she had, in fact, a burst appendix. Conditions were poor because of the snow and Daniel Mowat, a resident of Groats who had a big car, transported the poorly Bessie, along with her burst appendix, and the doctor directly to the hospital in Wick.

She was operated on right away, and the surgeon commented after the operation that she had not only had a burst appendix, but also an appendix abscess. If she hadn't had immediate medical attention she would have indeed just gone to sleep and died, her system was poisoned. Bessie, oblivious to her predicament, would have happily but ignorantly slept away.

Coincidently it transpired that there were two further admissions from John o' Groats at the same time to the local hospital, all with appendicitis.

Bessie was in hospital for ten days, and if she had wanted to be a nurse before she went into hospital she wanted it twenty times more now. She was just not destined to be working in a Post Office for the rest of her life. Fortunately for Bessie an opportunity eventually arose for her to take up an auxiliary nurse's post at the Henderson Home.
A woman from Groats had been admitted to the Henderson Home to have her baby, and the Matron in charge through conversation had asked her if she knew any young girls in her area who wanted to be nurses. Bessie's name jumped into her thoughts immediately, and she relayed it to the Matron.

Bessie is not sure whether the woman who had gone in to have her baby had mentioned to her mother that the hospital were looking for nurses, or the Matron had, in fact, telephoned Bessie's mother and asked if she was able to come to the Henderson for a position as an auxiliary nurse.

Whatever happened, Bessie was offered a position at the Henderson Home. The pay for this position was fifteen shillings a week, a large difference from the £2 regular pay she had been receiving from the Post Office. When the postmaster from Huna heard of Bessie's opportunity he offered her an increase in wages to £4 per week to stay on, which she declined.

Nothing, not even a large pay rise, was going to stop Bessie pursuing a career in nursing. This was her chance, and she was going for it and nothing was going to change her mind this time.

Chapter 2

The Nurse's Training

Bessie started at the Henderson Home in Wick when she was 19 years old and was delighted at becoming an auxiliary nurse and finally realising her calling. She made friends with another young girl, also named Elizabeth but Betty for short, who started at the same time. They both got on really well and worked at the Henderson for a year.

At that time, in order to get a place at a nursing school you had to join a list of potential applicants and wait for an opportunity to arise. This could be a lengthy process but as luck would have it not for the two girls, for after working at the Henderson for a year, the Matron at the home gave both girls a glowing reference to attend a nursing school in Aberdeen, and they were accepted right away.

The two girls could hardly believe that in no time at all they would be setting south to a new life with new experiences. Bessie felt a mixture of anxiety and excitement; she had never been a way from home before and wondered how she would feel being so far away from her mother and family. Nevertheless they set off to Aberdeen in 1947 and reported to the nurses' home, which would be their accommodation for the next three years. That year there were thirty-six nurses who started in Bessie's group.

The nurses' accommodation was very basic and contained a single bed, a chest of drawers and a wardrobe. This didn't really bother Bessie for she didn't need much room because she didn't have very much. The nurses received payment of 29 shillings and 11 pennies at the end of each month. Money was taken off for their accommodation, and what they received monthly was to purchase their own shoes and stockings and any other personal requirements.

The nurses' uniform consisted of a blue dress, white apron and starched white collar with a button to fix to the collar of their dress, and white cuffs. Additionally navy capes with red hoods were given, and a navy cardigan in case the weather was cold. Their uniform was to be pristine clean and worn correctly at all times. Bessie wondered if this was what the army was like, with uniforms being checked daily.

On top of their heads they wore frilly caps with a butterfly button. Black shoes and black stockings were the customary requirements, and if a run should occur in a stocking there was a shop nearby that did invisible mending. However stockings were very expensive so most of the time they were very careful not to snag them, or learned to darn them themselves with invisible thread.

Bessie as a trainee nurse

The maid's task was to give the trainee nurses an early morning call every day at 6.30am, as breakfast was served at 7am. Breakfast consisted of porridge, tea and toast which set them up for a long day of learning.

The first three months of the nurses' training consisted of attending lectures and learning everything concerned with medical, surgical, bacteriology, gynaecology and eyes, nose and throat. At the end of the three months a written house exam and an oral exam had to be completed and, on passing this, the nurses could then proceed to their next three months practical experience.

Bessie felt terribly homesick after she arrived in Aberdeen but once she got involved in her course she managed to cope well with being away from home. She spent her first three months in the overspill ward. This was a surgical ward, which, once a week, took any patients that Ward 9 could not accommodate. On passing her written and oral exam successfully she could then proceed onto the next part of her course. Thankfully Betty had also passed and both were delighted that they would carry on training together.

The following three months Bessie spent training in the diabetic and asthma ward, and then four other different wards after that. Bessie felt she was very lucky because a lot of nurses never gained the experience that she had been privy to.

They got one day off a week and ten days holiday in the year, which is when Betty and Bessie usually made their way north to Caithness, where Bessie spent her time back home with her family. Although it was hard living away from home, there were some perks. One of the nurses' fathers was a local fisherman and her mother would cook fresh cod roe and send it to the girls; this was one luxury that reminded them of home.

When Bessie got paid at the end of the month she and her colleagues would go out for a meal. This was a luxury as they didn't have the means to do it very often. When going out they would hope that they might identify a patient from the past who might recognise them and give them a cheaper deal due to their nursing care unfortunately this didn't happen very often.

One thing about nursing is that nurses are quite likely to catch an illness that patients have, and that was exactly what happened to Bessie whilst working in the eye ward. She woke up one day with a very sore throat. As doctors were always on hand in a hospital she asked one of them if they would have a look at her throat. At first the doctor thought that she might have diphtheria but, after further examination, it turned out that it was scarlet fever.

Bessie was directly transferred to the Aberdeen city hospital with a temperature of 105°C, and was put to bed immediately. As the maid came around at night with the tea trolley she asked Bessie if she'd like tea, coffee or cocoa, but all she wanted was a drink of water and even then a sip was all she could manage. Bessie was once again at the mercy of the medical staff as she lay in bed with not a care in the world.

The next time Bessie opened her eyes she noticed that she was surrounded by doctors and nurses dressed in gowns. "Good gracious," she thought, "Am I going to die?" She heard a woman's voice reassuring her and, as she turned towards her, she could see it was mother's sister. Bessie's Aunt Mary worked in the North British Hotel in Aberdeen, and was now sitting by her side and had been for some time.

It was at this point that Bessie thought she must be going to die. Why else would they all be looking so serious and have summoned her aunt to be with her? That night the doctor gave Bessie an injection with a needle the size of which she had never seen before in her life. She could hear them discussing the fact that the next twenty-four hours would be critical. Bessie knew that this was indeed really serious and wondered what would happen to her. However it must have done the trick, because the next morning when Bessie woke she felt as right as rain. The doctor said that he had never seen anyone recover so quickly before.

Bessie wasn't going to let a sore throat ruin her chances of becoming a nurse, not when she had got this far. She was made of stronger stuff; she had too much to lose. She came from a hardy family, born and bred in the windy tip of Scotland. Bessie continued to improve and wanted to get up but was told to be patient. As she continued to recover she was allowed to go home to Groats for the last ten days of her convalescing. Bessie's mother was glad to have her daughter home and made sure she was well enough before going back to her training.

Later it transpired that a woman whose family were suffering from scarlet fever had brought a bag to give to her husband who was in hospital for something else. Bessie had accepted the bag and, out of the eleven hundred staff at the hospital, Bessie and one other nurse contracted the scarlet fever. This was certainly not to be the last time Bessie would end up in her own ward.

The next time was when Sister noticed that Bessie was limping. "Nurse Manson, what is wrong with your foot?" she asked. Bessie told her she had an in-growing toenail, but that it wasn't too bad. Before Bessie had the chance to come on duty next day the hospital doctor had summoned her and on inspection informed her she would have to have her toenails removed. He arranged to have her toenails removed under a general anaesthetic the next day.

The operation rendered her unable to work for four weeks until she could walk properly again, as the feet have a lot to do with the balance of the body. As she had to have this operation it had resulted in her having a lot of time off work, so she had to make up three weeks night duty in order to complete her training time. At least she could sympathise with patients that had these disorders, as she had experienced them first hand herself.

Bessie's started a three-week night duty to make up the time she had lost and set off to a convalescent home in Hazelhead in Aberdeen. It was a big mansion house where there were two wards on the first floor and two on the second, both male and female. Staff slept on the third floor and the maid slept in the attic room. On arrival Bessie was met by Sister and given her instructions for her night on duty.

The house was very dark and none of the doors locked, but that didn't really bother her. There was a little maid who Bessie could only think resembled a little witch, with her bent back and chin that stuck out prominently. She was quite friendly though, and said "Hello dear. When you wake me in the morning my bed is against the door." Bessie looked at her in wonderment as she went on to say, "Because a nurse hung herself on that tree out there. You can hear the noises during the night".

This information did not fill Bessie with confidence and wondered if she would hear any noises during the night. Sister had informed her that her dinner was in the big Aga oven in the kitchen, and that she should eat at 1am. After the maid's revelation Bessie felt a bit nervous even though she had never experienced anything remotely like a ghost. The thought of having to go through this big spooky house to get her dinner made her uneasy. Instead of taking the long way around to the kitchen Bessie jumped over the kitchen hatch, got her dinner from the oven, climbed back through quickly, and sat down and ate it in the sitting room. She went through this ritual each night, as she didn't want to take any chances of hearing funny noises she couldn't explain.

One particular night she heard a bang, bang, like the sound of someone walking. Was this the ghost that the maid had warned her about and if so what would it look like. The maid had said she had been hung; however Bessie didn't want to imagine what she looked like. On investigation she found an old man wandering around saying his "quoits were yokit". Bessie propelled him back to bed without any cure, thinking that he was old and confused.

On translation from another nurse the next day it turned out his ankles had been itchy. Not knowing the local Aberdeenshire accent, Bessie had had no idea what he had meant. She had a lot to learn and was determined to do just that.

Two nights later Bessie saw a white figure coming along the corridor, she went up to the ward only to see that everyone was in bed. Was this a ghost this time she wondered, for she had never seen one? She had been sure the figure was that of a woman. Bessie wondered whether it was the nurse who had hanged herself. Did this mean that the maid was right? Was this the nurses ghost come back to haunt them? Bessie didn't generally believe in ghosts, but now she just wasn't too sure.

No, Bessie decided there had to be a reasonable explanation, so she went back to the ward and looked in again. She could see the slightest movement from one of the beds and went over to it. She lifted the cover, and underneath was an old woman looking up with wide eyes, wearing a man's white long johns and a white vest, with the purest white hair she had ever seen. The patient apologised for disturbing nurse, but she had needed to go to the toilet. Bessie was relieved, but also delighted that the vision had been, just as she had thought, a patient and not a ghost.

A further episode of Bessie's training that she will never forget involved the Sister's dogs. Sister had two beautiful spaniels that she doted on and Bessie had commented what nice dogs they were. Sister was pleased that Bessie felt that way about her dogs as she did. One night she asked Bessie if she would take them out for a walk in the woods next to the nursing home. Bessie agreed to take them, but once outside and seeing how dark it was she decided it would be safer if she just let them loose to run about the grounds.

Bessie's experience of dogs back home was that they just went about themselves, did their business, and came back and lay outside the back door. Thinking that this would probably be the same with the two spaniels she let them off their leads. The one thing she had not anticipated was that they would not come back on their own.

Bessie tried her best to get them to come back and shouted their names continually. She whistled and shouted again and again, but it was no use. She wondered what on earth she would do, and how she would explain the matter to the Sister. As it turned out there was no need, as Sister arrived outside the home and shouted to Nurse Manson within minutes. It transpired that the dogs had run up to the farm next door, and had proceeded to kill fifteen hens.

Bessie wondered how on earth Sister knew this; she informed her that the farmer had just phoned. Bessie didn't know how much compensation Sister had to pay the farmer for the hens but one thing was sure, she was never asked to walk her dogs again.

While Bessie carried out her month of night duty she had to stay in the Elms Hotel in Queen Street in Aberdeen. The one thing stipulated to her was that all nurses had to take a bus ride up and down Abbots Hill Road, and on no account to walk on their own, as the road was 1 ½ miles long. This route was regarded as unsafe for nurses to walk alone, especially at night. Two nurses were appointed to come and meet the bus and walk back to the home with the nurse on duty.

One particular night, though, Bessie had taken an earlier bus and had arrived ten minutes earlier than the scheduled meeting time. Bessie waited at the bus stop and listened for the nurses to come and meet her. She sensed that someone was behind her but didn't want to look round in case she drew attention to herself. She decided to walk towards the direction that she thought the nurses would be coming from, but as she quickened her steps she could hear the person's footsteps walking faster too. She slowed down and the footsteps slowed down. By this time Bessie was feeling a bit anxious and decided to cross the road into Cults. As she turned she could see a man cross the road and she followed him. She could see him hiding in the trees and peering through the leaves at her, so she made out she was leaving.

"Nurse Manson", a voice bellowed, "where have you been?" Bessie's heart lifted because she was so glad to see the nurses coming towards her, even if Sister looked annoyed. Sister continued, saying "In future you must come on the bus that you say you are coming on. Do you understand?"

Bessie fully understood the conditions, and made sure that the next night she got the bus that she had said she would and waited at the bus stop for the nurses. The next time she was aware of a car driving very slowly towards her, and Bessie started to feel anxious again. This time however it turned out to be one of the nurses with her boyfriend who had come to pick her up but the nurse couldn't get the window to wind down to shout to her. On realising it was safe Bessie jumped in the car and was delivered to the home safely in time for her shift.

The next day the daily papers published a story about a patient who had escaped from Wellwood Mental Hospital in Aberdeen.

Bessie assumed he must have been the man stalking her and hiding in the woods. It was the talk of the town and Bessie was relieved and grateful her experience had turned out the way it did for it could have been very different indeed.

Bessie was glad that her month at the convalescing home was coming to an end it had been quite a challenging 4 weeks to say the least. Unfortunately the nurse who was to come and relieve Bessie refused to come, probably due to hearing the ghost stories or escaping patients from mental hospitals, therefore she had to do another month until they could find someone else to take her place.

Finally back on duty in the main hospital once again, Bessie nearly received her first telling off, had it not been that Sister also had a sense of humour. One of the nurse's duties was to administer and empty patients' bedpans. Another trainee nurse was on duty with Bessie this day, and the rule was that they were only to carry two bedpans at a time.

As usual Bessie had learned to use her head to save her feet and carried three or four at a time. She had mastered a way of holding them to make sure they were secure. As she returned to the sluice room the other nurse on duty commented on how one of the female patients' skin around her "Penis" was very red. This particular patient had a plaster cast all round her body to help support her back and main body, and the edges were rubbing on her groin and this is why it was so red. The nurse had meant the patient's groin.

This particular nurse came from Aberdeen and from a well off background. Unfortunately her naivety let her down in the fact that she was unacquainted with the anatomy of men and, it seemed, women. This was worsened by the fact that the two nurses had both just attended anatomy and biology classes the previous day.

It was after the nurse's declaration about the female patient's redness that Bessie's hysteria returned, causing her to drop all the bedpans in her charge and bend over double with laughter. On hearing this commotion the ward sister came to find out what was wrong. Bessie was by this time unable to speak coherently, so the other nurse spoke to Sister and said she didn't know what was wrong with Nurse Manson, but she couldn't stop her laughing.

Sister ushered the hysterical Bessie into her office and asked her to explain what the problem was at once. Every time Bessie tried to tell her she laughed even more. Finally after a lot of breathing she managed to blurt out about the patient's redness and what the other nurse had called the woman's groin. At this point Sister doubled over with laughter too, which only fuelled Bessie's hysteria once again. She was eventually asked to leave the office and to get on with her work. How was Bessie ever to get over these bouts of laughter, if she ever would?

A further situation occurred with the same nurse, which would never be allowed to happen nowadays. One of the male patients had a detached retina and in those days the treatment for this was to lie in bed for nine months. This was a long time for a patient to lie and, to prevent bed sores occurring; they were regularly moved to new areas on the bed. This particular man required bed bathing and, as trained, both nurses were to start with the top of the body and arms, move down to the legs and feet and then do the middle of the patient's body. At all times they had to consider the patients modesty, and this was covered at all times with a towel.

As the nurses were bathing the patient something began to rise in his lower region. The nurse asked Bessie, "What is that?" Bessie, on looking to where the nurse was pointing, asked the nurse what she meant. She should have known what it was and Bessie thought she was trying to be smart.

On realising that she was not Bessie tried her best, in her own naivety, to explain to the nurse that a man gets feelings and, in turn, this makes changes in his body. The blank look from the nurse did nothing to reassure Bessie that this young girl knew any more, so she decided to leave it for the instructors who carried out their training to explain to this innocent girl.

Bessie could feel her self-control going again as the trainee nurse started to give the offending article a dicht (to tap) with her cloth. This of course only fuelled the intensity of the poor mans arousal as it increased in stature under the towel. Bessie couldn't look at the patient or the nurse any more and disappeared into the sluice room. Once Bessie had managed to compose herself enough to return to the ward the nurse had completed the patience's bed bath and left the ward still oblivious to the embarrassment she had just put the poor patient through.

You cannot say that all nursing tasks were dull, but Bessie wondered what would become of this young nurse if the simple things relating to the male anatomy were to rear their heads to her as a challenge in the future. Would she ever get married and god forbid she has any children.

On completing their training in 1951, Bessie, Betty and the rest of the nurses set out to celebrate the fact that they had sat their final exams. No one knew yet if they had passed, as they would only receive their certificates by post at a later date confirming if they would be a SRGN (State Registered General Nurse).

Bessie left Aberdeen in February and went back home to John O' Groats. There was no such thing as a graduation ceremony for them, unlike today, and all they could do was wait for their certificate to arrive by post, which happened within a few weeks. After getting their certificates Bessie and Betty decided to go on and do their midwifery training.

Out of the thirty six nurses who started training with Bessie only six went on to do their midder (Midwifery). Unfortunately they would have to go further south than Glasgow to do this, however they had heard that there was a new hospital at Irvine Central in Ayrshire. Bessie and Betty left the following June and headed to Ayrshire to do their midwife training, which was a one year course.

The first part of their training was carried out from theory learnt in tutorials. Practical tasks were carried out in taking blood pressures and palpating pregnant women's tummys to ascertain the way the baby was lying. Bessie loved working in the maternity wards, which reminded her, of when she would skip school one afternoon a week to go to the Henderson Home. The two nurses returned home just before Christmas for the holidays, and then returned to the Rob Roysten hospital in Glasgow for their next six months.

At Rob Royston Bessie was shown how to deliver babies, so most of her time was spent in the labour ward. One delivery that sticks in her mind was one birth that she had to deliver alone. Normally this would not be a problem, but there had been a problem with both the lights and the baby. She was standing in darkness delivering this woman's baby and it turned out that it was a stillbirth. This in itself was quite distressing particularly since the baby was born without a brain. The doctors had anticipated this very sad delivery already. They knew that this baby would not survive, and this may have been a reason why Bessie was allowed to carry out the delivery on her own.

This would be very unlikely to happen nowadays, as anencephalic babies are not common. Another part of Bessie's duties in the hospital was to scrub the sheets in the sluice room that were used in the labour wards. Washing machines were non-existent in those days, so elbow grease and a good scrubbing brush were the order of the day.

Although Bessie had worked in the sluice room several times she had never really taken much notice of her surroundings, until one day she noticed that there was a big jar containing a small baby with two heads. Bessie was intrigued by this vision, as she had never seen anything like it before. Sister informed her that these were conjoined twins, and that they had been born alive. Both heads had cried but they had died shortly after.

An additional jar in the room held the body of another baby who had three eyes, three arms and three legs. This was another example of a conjoined set of twins which had died once born. It was sad that in those days these abnormalities were not detected sooner, without causing so much pain and suffering to both mother and child.

Another day Bessie was working away in the sluice room when she heard what sounded like a baby's cry. She went over to the heap of linen and looked underneath, thinking the sound was coming from a radiator situated at the window. Much to Bessie's surprise, on lifting the linen she felt something in it. When she unfolded it she discovered a baby, very much alive with a good pair of lungs by the level of noise coming from it. Shocked and amazed by her discovery and unsure what to do, Bessie wrapped the baby in a clean towel, ran upstairs to the labour ward and presented the live baby to the Sister on duty. "Look what I just found", she said to Sister in disbelief.

The look on the Sister's face was somewhere between disbelief, embarrassment and anger. "Don't you dare tell anyone about this", she said under her breath and grabbed the baby from her. Bessie discovered later that Sister had already broken the news to the mother and father that the baby had died during birth, and she then had to go and tell him that in fact his baby was very much alive. Bessie would have liked to have been a fly on the wall when Sister had to break the news to the couple.

One explanation could have been that sometimes when a baby is born they are very flat, and it is difficult for them to come around as quickly as normal babies usually do. It was indeed a mistake that the baby was wrapped up in the linen from the bed and sent to the sluice room. One theory was that since the baby was set near a radiator the heat may have revived it. There was no real explanation as to how the baby came to be in the sluice room, and Bessie never found out who did it or why it happened as it was never mentioned again.

Once a nurse had experience in the labour ward they were sent to an administration room in Rotten Row in Glasgow. All the district nurses congregated there and when a call came in for a midwife they would go by taxi or bus to the address given and deliver the baby, then return to the administration room and wait for another call.

Bessie's training meant that she delivered babies out in the Gorbals of Glasgow which was a poorer area that did not always have a good reputation. However to Bessie a baby was a baby wherever it was born and she loved being a midwife. One aspect that always struck Bessie was the kindness and generosity of these poorer people. Despite the fact they didn't have much there was always a cup of tea offered to the nurse, even if it was in a jam jar. Most of the houses had a TV, a packet of Woodbine and an army blanket thrown over a straw palyass (mattress). The folk didn't have much, but were content enough with their lot.

Knits Hill however was a new housing scheme in Glasgow and a bit more upmarket than her usual district, but Bessie had to go to a delivery in this area one day. Whilst having no luck in finding the address given she stopped and asked an old bent woman how to get there. She told her to get the 48A bus and sure enough, to Bessie's surprise, it took her to the right address. Bessie had been at this pregnant woman's house from 10am until 5pm and was never once offered a drink of tea, in total contrast to her treatment in her usual area.

Whilst the trainee midwives were allowed to go to the pregnant woman's house, they still had to wait for a midwife to oversee their delivery. On this occasion the overseeing midwife arrived and asked Bessie if she had had anything to eat or drink all day. When Bessie answered that she hadn't the midwife asked the mother of the pregnant woman if she could possibly give the young nurse a cup of tea. The woman went off to make her tea and brought two slices of toast, which were very hot with butter dripping off them when she returned.

Bessie was famished and very grateful for the food, and ate it quickly before delivering the woman's baby. Returning to the administration room Bessie proceeded to throw up as she was getting off the bus. The hot toast with lashings of melted butter had just been too much for Bessie's empty stomach that day.

During their training the nurses were always told that the most important thing, next to delivering a healthy baby, was the checking of the afterbirth. The afterbirth had to be examined for the five lobes which it was made up of, to make sure it was complete. If not the nurse had to wait to make sure the mother had passed it all.

In some cases, by the time that Bessie got to the pregnant women they would have had their babies and flushed the afterbirth down the toilet, which made her job more difficult. Bessie always thought that the afterbirth reminded her of liver; which were taken back and disposed of in the hospital incinerator.

As Irvine Central was a brand new hospital there was a pristine large Milton tank just for the babies' bottles, holding around 30-40 bottles at a time. It had to be filled with fresh water and

Milton sterilising fluid every day, and this particular day it was Bessie's turn in the Milton room. A single tap filled the Milton tank, but the force of water from the tap wasn't very high so the nurses were told to go and do other jobs while it filled up.

Bessie couldn't be bothered to wait for the tank to fill up, so she went off to do other duties whilst it was filling. As Bessie was on a split shift she finished at three o' clock and had to return at five. When Bessie went back on duty Sister was waiting at the door for her with a stern look on her face. Bessie wondered why she looked so disgruntled but didn't have to wait long to find out.

"Do you realise that the Head Surgeon had to wear Wellington boots to get upstairs, Nurse Manson?" Bessie wondered why on earth the surgeon would have required to be wearing Wellington boots, and of what relevance it was to her anyway. Then it dawned on Bessie that she had forgotten to return to the Milton room before going off duty, and the water had been running all afternoon. It had flooded the room and surrounding corridors. She never did that again!

Bessie was delivering a woman's baby one day when the husband came into the labour ward to be with his wife. Bessie's experience had shown that some husbands were overcome with the smell of anaesthetic or the sight of blood, and frequently passed out. As her full attention had to be on the birth of the baby and the care of the mother, Bessie would reiterate to the husband that if he felt sick or dizzy he should sit down on the floor until he felt better.

During the delivery tere was a loud thud. As Bessie was in the middle of delivering the baby she took no notice, it was nothing involving the mother, baby or midwife, so she disregarded the event. Once the baby was born the woman asked where her husband was and, as Bessie looked to the area where he should have been standing, he was nowhere to be seen.

43

However, as she glanced down on the floor she could see him lying full length out cold.

When he came to he was lying on a bed in a cubicle having his eye stitched up, whilst his wife was in the labour ward having her stitches put in after having her baby. It didn't matter how many times Bessie prepared these men they never let her down as they keeled over at the least wee thing.

Bessie enjoyed working in Glasgow but hated the food. The nurses didn't get out very often, so one day Bessie and another nurse seized an opportunity to go on a trip to Prestwick Airport near Glasgow.

They had heard that the biggest bomber, the Brabazon, was arriving at Prestwick airport, and Bessie and her colleague decided to go out and see it land. They arrived at the airport and made their way to the runway where they were told to get off by a very angry policeman. They had no fear and thought it was a great sight to see all the men disembark the plane with their hard hats and uniforms on.

They also went to the pictures to see the film called "White Corridors" showing in the local cinema. The story was about a doctor who worked in a hospital, which was involved in the making of a new drug. The doctor took the drug himself and experienced all the effects of it to see if it was okay for other patients. He risked his own life to save others, and survived. He was indeed a hero as well as a good looker and all the young nurses thought this is what a real doctor is like.

Another day off Bessie and another nurse borrowed some bikes and cycled out to Largs, about thirty miles from Irvine Central, for the day. They set off in the early morning after coming straight off night duty. It took them a few hours to get there, but was quite effortless as they were used to cycling.

The first thing that impressed Bessie on arrival at Largs was the Viking Picture House, which was in the shape of a Viking ship. Whilst there Bessie took the opportunity to go out in a speedboat and have a run around the harbour, which cost just one shilling.

In a way the experience of the sea reminded her of home and made her feel a bit closer to her family. When the girls were nearly three quarters of the way back to Irvine Central tiredness overtook them, for they had come off night duty that morning and had never slept.

It was at that moment, as they were both resting at the side of the road, that Bessie noticed a lorry going past with two young men in it. She beckoned to the lorry driver, who pulled in to the side of the road. Bessie's colleague was embarrassed by the situation and berated Bessie for stopping the lorry, for they knew nothing about these two young men. Bessie told her not to be so daft as they were just young boys, that nothing was going to happen to them, and that in any event there was no way they could cycle any further.

The two boys put the girls' bikes in the back of the lorry and drove them to Irvine Central. On arrival they took the bikes out of the lorry and returned them to the nurses. The only thing the boys wanted in return for their kind gesture was a photo of the two girls beside the lorry with them.

The two girls eventually went to bed and slept for twenty-four hours. This only illustrates once again the fact that Bessie still hadn't a care in the world, and no sense of fear. She looked at life the same way as she had done at home. In this day and age that outing could have had a completely different result.

Chapter 3

Getting Married

Bessie had known her prospective Stroma husband for many years but had always kept him at arms length, as she didn't really want to settle down and get married until she had finished her nurses training. Every time Bessie came home on leave Sinclair would make his way over from the island of Stroma to visit her. Bessie had very little leave at home and Sinclair, being a fisherman, worked with the tides, so there were few occasions for courting.

Stroma was a small island just north of Groat's surrounded by the treacherous waters of the Pentland Firth. The flood tide runs east from the Atlantic Ocean to the North Sea and the Stroma men had to be well experienced in the rushing tides. Sinclair would set off from Stroma in his Stroma Yawl, the Victory across the short stretch of water landing at the Huna Pier just to spend the little time with Bessie.

One particular night in 1951, it was very windy; this was nothing unusual on Stroma, as even severe gales could occur without having any impact at all. This particular night, though, everyone on the island was in bed when the wind got up and was particularly strong, in the early hours of the morning. When the Stroma residents arose in the morning all they could see around them was complete devastation.

The wind had certainly blown. It had blown so hard that all hen houses on the island had been completely lost, for there was nowhere for them to go but into the sea. Countless hens were found lying dead about the island. Some, fortunately, were found alive in ditches but a vast amount of poultry was lost that year, and from the nearby Orkney Islands too.

The times the couple had together were very precious indeed. Sinclair took Bessie boating on the Wick River one gala week, and short visits to Stroma when the weather was good filled some of their precious time together.

Other social events on Stroma included whist drives in the local school in the winter time. Concerts and dances in the winter and summer were popular; in some instances people came across from the Mainland to a Stroma dance. Sailing model yachts on the loch was a competitive pastime, and Sinclair's father sailed his model yacht the Eclipse in both the summertime and winter. Sometimes the Stroma men would travel over to the Sarclet Loch in Caithness, just outside Wick, for local competitions. Sinclair's father won a lot of prizes for sailing, including a cup.

Bessie is still, to this day, surprised at how long she made Sinclair suffer and wait for her, with her devil-may-care attitude to life.
It was when she was home on leave, on the 29th December 1951, that Sinclair plucked up the courage to ask this young nurse to marry him. Sinclair was a quiet, unassuming man, and not one to show his feelings publicly. He had taken Bessie out to the Rosebank Hotel in Wick to have a special meal when, to Bessie's surprise, he presented her with an engagement ring and asked her to marry him.

There was nothing unusual about their getting engaged, as Sinclair had made it obvious to Bessie that he had indeed cared for her for many years. It was the fact that Sinclair would only put the ring on her finger under the table, so no one would see them, which showed the full extent of his bashfulness. Sinclair was a very private man, but he was very happy indeed when Bessie agreed to marry him. They set a date for the following December.

Bessie returned to Rob Royston after New Year, to complete the second part of her midwifery training, showing off a lovely new engagement ring. One day she had taken if off to wash her hands and it just popped down the plughole before she had a chance to catch it. Distraught, Bessie got one of the staff to retrieve it from the plumbing, which was very lucky indeed for her. After that Bessie took more care of her precious engagement ring.

Bessie completed her Midwifery training and returned home just before the summer of 1952. She was offered a post in the Henderson Home as a sister on night shift, back where she had started before setting off for her training five years previously. As she prepared for her impending wedding in December she continued to work at the Henderson until late November 1952.

Bessie far left and other nurses with sister in middle

Bessie regularly attended the Wee Free Kirk in Canisbay, near John o' Groats, and this was where they would be married. Bessie's mother was to arrange for the minister to marry them and, as the current Wee Free minister was not ordained and wouldn't get his collar for several months, she took on the services of Minister MacPhee from the Baptist Kirk in Scarfskerry, several miles from Groats. Bessie's mother, being a kindly person, then wondered if the minister from the Canisbay Church (Queen Mothers Church) would feel left out, so she decided to ask all three ministers to attend her daughter's wedding.

Bessie bought her wedding dress from Mowats the draper shop in Wick. It was a beautiful white brocade dress with a square neck, which cost about £14, with white satin shoes to go with it. She had also bought her going away outfit, a light green checked suit which had cost £10 in Glasgow, which she had bought before coming home at the end of her training. Bessie's wedding flowers were white chrysanthemums and red roses. The cake had three tiers and came from the Cliff Bakery in Wick. The reception was to cost £44 for a two-course dinner and dance for all 180 people attending at the John o' Groats Hotel.

When preparing for her wedding Bessie's sister in law asked her if she had white tights. When Bessie replied that she didn't, she told her to pop a normal skin-coloured pair into some bleach, and that would take the colour out and make them white. This would look better under her white dress. Prepared with this valuable information Bessie steeped the brown tights in watered bleach overnight.

When she took the tights out of the solution in the morning all she was left with were bits she could only compare to segments of a tapeworm, as the bleach had burnt the tights to pieces. Bessie had thought she was to leave them overnight, but this was not the case. A dip in and out would have been sufficient. Not one to be fazed by such a happening, Bessie wore her brown tights as usual under her beautiful white dress with her white shoes. Well, she thought, no one would notice.
Bessie did her own hair for her wedding. Not tin curlers this time, but plastic rollers. She set her hair with setting lotion and kept the curlers in overnight. I can only imagine the pain of placing a head covered in the prickly rollers on a pillow.

Bessie, however thought this a small price to pay to look good for her big day.

When Sinclair and Bessie left Stroma on the Tuesday before the wedding a couple gave them a little white lame pot with a handle, which was half filled with salt. They wished them all the best as this was supposed to be very lucky. Bessie often thought of them later on in life when the bairns used it as a little chanty.

The couple married on 12th December in 1952 at the Wee Free Kirk in Canisbay at 7pm, well it was actually a bit later than that. The wedding was late because Bessie's mother couldn't shut the post office until then. Because she had to man the phone twenty-four hours a day she had asked a local gentleman to watch over the phone all night to let her get away to the wedding. When he arrived Bessie's mother told him she had made some dinner for him, and that it was on the cooker. As he went to pick it up it slipped from his hand and fell down the back of the cooker. Bessie, once again ready to give in to impending laughter, begged her mother to come right away and leave him to sort it out himself.

As Bessie left home for the church it emerged that the groom and best man had no buttonholes, as they had been left at the post office, Bessie wondered whether anything more could go wrong. Eventually, buttonholes in hand, Bessie and her brother headed for the Kirk. Someone met them and rushed the buttonholes to the groom and best man before the bride entered the Kirk. Before the wedding Bessie had asked her oldest brother, who was a tall man, to walk slowly as they walked down the aisle, because she wanted to keep up with him. However Bessie felt she was in a marathon, as they nearly ran down the aisle to where the groom and ministers stood.

As she joined her husband-to-be at the pew, they faced the three ministers standing together in the pulpit. Sinclair was a bit surprised at being married by three ministers, but thought he'd better go along with it anyway. He'd never been married before, so what did he know? They certainly did things in style on the mainland he thought, silently.

They both stood together alongside their bridesmaids and best man as Minister MacPhee carried out the wedding ceremony, and the two other ministers looked on. Bessie and Sinclair took their vows in front of the congregation, and were duly pronounced man and wife.

The three ministers, bride, groom, best man, bridesmaid and maid of honour then made their way to the vestry, to the traditional signing of the register. Everyone duly signed the register except for the bride and groom. Bessie thought this was strange and mentioned this to Sinclair, but as neither had ever been in a vestry before they assumed that this must be how it was done. In view of the fact that they had taken their vows in the presence of God the two newlyweds never gave it another thought.

Once the couple were married everyone made their way to the John o' Groats hotel to enjoy the wedding reception. For the meal there was no starter, unless anyone wanted fruit juice, chicken was served for the main course, and dessert was trifle and ice cream followed by coffee and cake. Once the speeches were made, following the usual "On behalf of my wife and I" where everyone cheered, the night got away to a good start.

The traditional wedding march was performed, and afterwards the local band played traditional Scottish music, with the odd song sung by local folk. Bessie remembers one man who sang a song to her called "The Bonnie Lass of Balloch mile".

As the night wore on Sinclair became increasingly aware that the Stroma crowd would be keen to make mischief for the newly weds, so he had arranged for one of the local men to drive him and Bessie to Wick before anything untoward could happen. Bessie and Sinclair arranged to meet separately so no one would suspect they were leaving together, at the wee shed near the hotel, where their driver would meet them.

Bessie made her way to the agreed meeting point and could see Sinclair pacing up and down outside the shed, but no sign of the driver. Eventually he arrived, a little the worse for wear. They headed off to the Rosebank Hotel in Wick, even though it took them twice as long as normal due to the driver veering from side to side of the road most of the way.

Bessie and Sinclair spent their wedding night in the Rosebank Hotel, and were planning to head off the next day to Edinburgh for their honeymoon.

Unfortunately they were weather bound, and no planes or trains could get out of Caithness. It was the Tuesday after their wedding before they managed to get a train to Edinburgh. They stayed in a guesthouse which was cold with no hot water for a week, and then made their way up to Aberdeen to stay with friends for another week.

On returning home to Caithness the local paper had an announcement, "Stroma fisherman takes a wife. Problem solved for resident nurse".

Mary Steven was Bessie's great Granny, and the story goes that she was the *first* bride to come from John o' Groats to Stroma. As it turned out, Bessie was to be the *last* bride to come from Groats to Stroma.

Bessie and Sinclair cutting their wedding cake

Chapter 4

Sailing Home

After the honeymoon Bessie moved her belongings from her old home in John O' Groats to Stroma, which was to be her new home. They both made the journey over the three miles of the Pentland Firth, one of the most treacherous straits in Britain, in Sinclair's Stoma Yawl. For the time being she and Sinclair were to live with his parents, and Bessie didn't mind at all because Sinclair's mother was a gem. Bessie liked her very much and they came to be very good friends.

It was shortly after moving that Bessie received a letter from the Medical Committee asking if she would be interested in taking up the post of District Nurse on Stroma. Her wages were to be £8 per week. Accommodation was provided at the nurse's cottage, where the furnishings included a three-legged table and a bed settee with a hump in the middle, for £1 a week. Bessie accepted the job right away, and began her married life with Sinclair and her new post as District Nurse. The nurse's cottage was their home until Sinclair's mother took ill and they moved into Glencairn to look after her.

Campbell Shearer was Bessie's great-great Grandmother, and was the 'Howdy', or midwife, for John o' Groats and the surrounding parish. She delivered over eleven hundred babies. The local Minister got her trained locally. Bessie remembers hearing a story about a woman who had awful pains in her stomach. It turned out that her brother had had his wicked way with her, and she had a child to her brother.

Bessie loved Stroma and worked as the district nurse day and night. There were no limits to working hours in this job, especially when you lived on an island. You were on call 24 hours a day. With an ageing population there were many people to check on daily.

The nurse's work was much more diverse than you would think. Some people thought that because Bessie had medical knowledge she could conduct any medical procedure, perhaps even carrying out veterinary practices.

Bessie and Sinclair centre back in Stroma

One day a neighbour came running in, shouting "Come quick nurse, his insides are hanging oot". As Bessie grabbed her medical bag she was fearful for the woman's husband, wondering what on earth he could have done to get such an injury. She was methodically going through all the procedures in her mind for this type of accident, such as making sure all entrails were lathered in antiseptic lotion and accounted for. As she rushed up the road she wondered how much blood the man would have lost, and how she could get it made up quickly. On entering the house imagine her surprise when she saw the woman's husband safe, holding their sheep dog in a tin bath whilst blood was running out of its belly. Bessie felt both relief and disbelief at the sight in front of her.

She immediately told the woman to go and get a bag of flour, which she quickly administered to the belly of the dog and wrapped the wound with an old shirt. Eventually the bleeding stopped, and the dog was weak but stable. The tear was stitched up, thanks to Bessie's sewing skills learnt at school, and antiseptic administered to the wound. Typical of Bessie's caring nature she returned the following day to check on the animal. As Bessie left the woman gave her some baking as a gesture of goodwill, which Bessie accepted with gratitude.

A previous medical emergency occurred a short time before Bessie married. She had come over to the island to stay with Sinclair's sister for the night. His brother-in-law, had come in to see Sinclair's father, as one of his stirks, or young cows, had cut a main artery in its nose on a fence and was bleeding profusely. There was no way the vet could come across from the mainland in time and they thought they would lose the beast. As usual Bessie offered to come and help but, by the time they got to him the stirk had lost so much blood it was down on its knees.

On seeing the plight of this helpless animal Bessie told Sinclair's brother-in-law to go and get some turpentine and one of the bairn's nappies. She cleaned away all the blood clots from the stirk's nose, and took turpentine and cotton wool and shoved it up his nose then wrapped it with a terry nappy, binding it round his nose. She then put a bottle of salted water to replenish some of the blood he'd lost. She told Sinclair's brother-in-law that it would take time, but they would know after twenty-four hours if the stirk would be okay.

The next morning Sinclair's brother-in-law came into the house and Bessie asked how the stirk was. He said it was much better, but was unable to eat as the nappy was bound around its mouth so tightly. Bessie told him to snip the corners just enough to allow it to get its mouth open to eat, but not to remove the binding. This he did and the stirk made a full recovery, so much so that it was later sold at the mart for a considerable amount of money.

The local health board would regularly send their superintendents to visit the district nurses and go on their rounds with them, whilst taking stock of their duties. On the visit to Stroma Bessie took the superintendent around with her and showed her what she did on a daily basis.

The Superintendent asked Bessie, "Why don't you come to Edinburgh and learn to do your Queens? You could learn to drive and get a licence." Bessie said she would think about it and discuss it with her husband. Later she mentioned to Sinclair what the woman had suggested. Sinclair had trained as a wireless operator in the Merchant Navy and if he also did a further short training course as a civilian he would get better pay. The prospect of doing a further six months training didn't seem too long to either Bessie or Sinclair, for they had no responsibilities. However, after much deliberation they decided against it as they had Sinclair's ailing parents to look after. Once again her sense of duty prevented Bessie from following her ideal career path.

Although Bessie had trained as a midwife, there was only one woman pregnant in the five years she was nurse on the Island. The woman had to go across to the mainland because of complications anyway, so she never actually delivered any babies on Stroma.

Food was always plentiful on the island, as the neighbours shared any animals that were slaughtered. Many residents would rear a pig on the island, feeding it up until it was ready for slaughter. Once killed it was distributed amongst neighbours and, shortly afterwards, another neighbour's pig would be ready for slaughter. Pork was salted in a barrel, but not in large quantities as sharing with neighbours meant there was a constant supply of fresh pork.

Mutton, lamb, chicken, fish and partins (or crab) was a nourishing diet for any community. The women milked the cows, made butter and had eggs a-plenty. The surplus went to the local shop and, if there was more than even they needed then the rest was despatched to the mainland for sale.

Despite being a midwife Bessie had visions of having a family too and as her first-born was due soon she had to go across the Pentland Firth to stay with her mother for a week, as she was not expected to deliver her own baby.

Whilst back at her childhood home Bessie helped her mother with some cleaning to pass the time away. Her mother had an Elsinel, (dry) toilet and Bessie decided to give it a good clean. Whether this had an affect on the timely arrival of the baby we'll never know, however the next morning Bessie woke up to find her waters breaking, and was duly sent into the home in preparation of the baby's birth. Matron administered Bessie with castor oil, as was the practice then, and told her to have a hot bath. This indeed had the desired effect and a fine strapping boy was born the next day, on April 9th 1954. He was named William Bremner after his grandfather. This baby was to be the first of many to complement Bessie and Sinclair's family.

Sinclair and Bessie holding William

Chapter 5

No Sense of Direction

Bessie had no sense of direction and Sinclair's father had always told her that if she followed the moon, she would always find her way about on the island. However, to Bessie the moon was just a light in the sky and nothing more. Sinclair, as well as being a fisherman, was also an auxiliary coastguard on the island and frequently had to do night duty at the look out.

One evening he told Bessie to come up and visit him, as he was on duty, and have a cup of tea. He told her to take the shortcut home across the heather, between the nurse's home and Glencairn, but she was so scared she would end up in the Gloup, which was a deep hole in the land that she took the long way home instead.

The weather always had an impact on the way things were on an island, because if the weather was bad no one could go across to the Mainland for stores, etc. One day in 1953 there was a particularly stormy day, Bessie asked Sinclair to nip up and see if his mother and father were okay. So he jumped on the bike and, as Bessie watched him he faced his bike in the direction of Glencairn his parents house. She saw that his feet never touched the pedals as the wind propelled him up the road, right past his parent's house, and straight into the ditch opposite.

The corn screws were in a precarious state with the wind, so Sinclair and his brother-in-law went to try and secure them. They lifted a sleeper to set on top of one screw, but before they had got it off the ground the corn screw took off like paper and blew away. There was little the two men could do as their winter fodder took off and flew across the fields into the stormy Pentland Firth.

Bessie's navigational skills did not improve even in daylight. In the winter of 1954, there was a particularly heavy snowfall and the ground was knee deep in snow. The weather had been especially severe. Sinclair's father had broken his leg.

It was a pathological fracture. He had been in bed for a year with high blood pressure, and when he got up his leg had broken. As it was not suitable weather for him to be taken off the island by boat and ambulance to the hospital he had to be uplifted by a helicopter. The rescue operation was fittingly called "Operation Snowdrop".

Bessie wanted to check that the heating was okay, in this particularly snowy weather, at the nurse's cottage. She thought if she followed the telegraph poles from Glencairn to the cottage she would be fine. So, Bessie donned her Wellington boots, gloves and thick coat, ready to face the deep blanket of snow. She set off across the land but, as the snow was so deep, she couldn't even see the loch. As Bessie came to the second-last telegraph pole before the nurse's cottage she sank, and her wellies filled up with a sudden gushing of water.

As Bessie held on tight to the telegraph pole she wondered if she would be found drowned in this big main water ditch. She eventually managed to crawl out of the ditch, and then ran the rest of the way to the nurse's cottage. Once inside the cottage she danced on the floor until she got the feeling back in her numb legs.

On her return to Glencairn, still frightened she would fall in the loch; instead of going back the way she had come she crawled up the road side of the telegraph poles until she got back.

Bessie was a well-known face among the community of Stroma and loved the island life. Although she had a young family of her own she continued to carry out her nurse's duty, and would set off with the baby wrapped up well in his pram. She would make her daily calls, checking on everyone as usual, but had never anticipated that a large majority of her community would be fighting over the chance to look after the baby while she went about her work.

Bessie had no driving licence but this did not deter her from driving the Jeep. Sinclair had purchased the left-hand-drive Jeep from a man in Gills, a few miles up the road from Groats, for £25, which never put Bessie up or down. She drove about the island quite content with her four wheels.

Two Stroma residents had taken in a woman and her son from London during the Blitz. The woman was going away back to London, and Bessie was asked to deliver the woman and her son to the Haven with her luggage to catch the boat. She did this, and then drove back home, where she received a severe telling off from her father-in-law. He told her she was very irresponsible driving down there with the Jeep, as someone had gone down there and had driven over the edge.

Bessie just thought he was overreacting, however the next day when Sinclair took the Jeep to another part of the island the brakes gave in. Luckily he was not hurt, nor did the Jeep get damaged. As Bessie reflected on this information she thought of her delivery of the woman to the Haven and the steep brae. Things certainly could have easily resulted in disaster.

Bessie wasn't even safe on two wheels never mind four. It was very late one evening as she set off on her bicycle to one of her patients. This particular patient had a tendency to wander at night. She was pedalling down between Glencairn and the nurse's home when she hit a bump in the road, pitched over the handlebars of her bike, and landed face down in the ditch. Stunned by her fall, but eager to get to her patient, she left the offending bike where it lay and ran onto her patient's house, picking the bike up on her way back home.

It wasn't long before Bessie's second child was due and, as before, Bessie was despatched to her mother's to have her baby. The night before the baby was born Bessie had walked the long road up to Duncansby Head from the John o' Groats Post Office, and along the cliffs to see the ship *Euceles* which had run aground just off the Stacks of Duncansby. Predictably, a baby girl was born the next day at the Henderson home in Wick, on the 9th Day of December 1955. Elizabeth Isabella was fittingly named after her mother and grandmother. Bessie returned home to Stroma with another little bundle and continued with her work, despite now having two young children and a husband to look after.

The district nurse was issued with a medical bag in which were syringes, for taking blood tests and administering medicine, whisky, in case anyone passed out, M&V tablets, painkillers, and lint.

One of the lighthouse keeper's daughters aged nine or ten years, had an embarrassing itch. On investigation Bessie discovered she had a round worm in her intestine. In this case the young girl was fortunate to pass the worm after two or three days.

When Bessie was doing her training they simply fed the patients who had round worms, and had to keep checking after they had gone to the toilet. If the head of the worm had been passed then that was okay, if not they had to keep checking with a stick every time until it was passed.

Another of the lighthouse keeper had contracted malaria, which reoccurred and had tablets to take when he had a bad turn. Unfortunately his four-year-old daughter had eaten two of the malaria tablets by mistake, and Bessie had to keep an eye on her for a few days. Luckily, as it turned out, she was okay.

Bessie dealt with every-day occurrences, and visited everyone on the island. She would go to see her patients, whilst William and Elizabeth would be amused by the old folk playing spoons. If the fishermen had boils she would go to them and give them penicillin injections. Boils were sore and difficult to get rid of.

In some instances Bessie had to remove the inside of the boil, which would unfortunately leave scarring, but the removal of the boil would be worth it to some.

Nurses were not permitted to catheterise a man but, as the local doctor couldn't get to the island, Bessie had no option but to do it. This level of independence was not unusual. Another resident had rheumatic fever and all his joints were sore, however the doctor only visited once or twice during his whole illness, so Bessie had to use her own discretion in treating the patient.

One resident had fleabitus on his leg and Bessie put on a kaolin poultice to take out the infection, which caused inflammation of the superficial tissue. Bessie sometimes had to improvise and do what she thought was right, if the doctor couldn't get over to the island because of weather conditions.

Bessie also had a drugs cabinet, in order to administer medicines such as penicillin, and painkillers which she ordered from the chemist. It was sent over in a special cabinet to keep it secure until she received it safely.

Bessie continued her rounds until baby number three was due for delivery. She was despatched, as usual, to her mother's until she was ready to go to the Home. Once again Bessie, not being one to lie about the house, decided to walk up to the Duncansby Head Lighthouse to visit a friend.

Her friend had been baking meringues, and Bessie couldn't contain her craving for them. After consuming seven meringues her friend asked her, "If that baby is born tomorrow will you call it Meringue?" Bessie laughed at the suggestion, for she had already promised her aunt Mary that she would call the child after her if it was a girl. Bessie lay in bed later that night wondering if this baby would be a boy or girl.

She awoke in the early morning feeling a desperate need to go to the toilet. As she made her way to the Elsinel toilet at the back of the house she heard her mother call, "Are you all right, buddo?" Bessie said she was fine, and that she just needed to go to the toilet. However on her way back she asked her mother to call the nurse, as she was indeed in full-blown labour. She went back through and lay on her bed awaiting the arrival of the local Nurse. As Bessie lay waiting she heard the nurse arrive, and her mother telling the nurse to take her coat off, sit down and have some breakfast.

Bessie shouted through, "Hurry up if you want to deliver this baby". The Nurse replied, "You nurses, you're all the same". As the nurse rounded the door Bessie had no option but to push and, at that moment, Mary Sinclair (Marion for short, I suppose it *does* sound a bit like meringue) was born. At 8am on the 26th February 1957, with no time to get to the Henderson for delivery. Bessie felt a twang of disappointment to have missed her castor oil and her hot bath,"what a shame", she thought as she smiled to herself.

On returning to Stroma Bessie now had three children to look after and, indeed, had her hands even more full. However, she still had a duty to carry out her work, even though she had gone down to part-time hours.

On the island there was a family consisting of two sisters, one with a child, and a brother. One of them had asked Bessie what they could take to cure constipation, because they all had a touch of it. Bessie told them to take a teaspoon of liquid paraffin each day until they noticed a difference. A few days later Bessie met the minister on her rounds, and he notified her that she had nearly killed them.
Bessie, shocked by this revelation, went to visit them immediately out of concern. She couldn't understand how her advice could possibly have made them so ill. Could they have taken too much? Bessie asked the woman to show her what

she had taken, and she showed Bessie the liquid. Bessie was astounded to realise it was paraffin oil.

Marion, William and Elizabeth Bremner

Bessie explained to the woman that this was not what she had told her to take, this was paraffin oil. She told the woman it was liquid paraffin she had been supposed to take. The woman looked at Bessie and agreed, "That's what it is, paraffin liquid." Bessie couldn't get the woman to understand that these two things were not the same. One thing that it had done was to rectify their constipation, albeit not in the recommended way.

The same family had gas installed to their house as an alternative to electricity. A lot of the islanders were having this done at that time. A few days later, on her rounds, Bessie entered the house only to get a strong smell of gas. When she mentioned this to the household the woman said that she didn't think much of this new fuel, because it didn't last long at all.

On investigating further it turned out that the gas had been turned on, and had since been leaking continually. Unfortunately the woman didn't understand how gas worked, and thought that if she blew it out after she had finished using it then it would automatically be turned off. Bessie reflected that the only thing that had saved them from the ill effects of inhaling the gas fumes was the ventilation provided by the old draughty window in the kitchen.

When visiting people in their homes it was traditional that men always got a nip of whisky, and women got a cup of tea. As Bessie was visiting the same family, she became uncomfortable when one of the sisters laid a filthy towel on her knee in preparation for giving her a piece of cake. As if that were not bad enough, the woman's hands were filthy. Then Bessie had to sit and drink her tea, even though she could see that the woman had lice crawling over her. When Bessie got home she had to steep her clothes before washing them, to be sure they were properly clean. It was from experiences such as these that Bessie realised that this family were unable to look after themselves properly and recommended that they get help.

One task that Bessie didn't particularly like was once a resident passed away she had to dress the body in readiness for the impending funeral. As was the customer when a couple got married the wife always made a shirt for the husband to get married in and then it was kept for when they passed on. One particular gentleman had died and Bessie had to go and prepare the body for the funeral. She enlisted the help of her brother- in-law to help clothe the man. As was the custom she brought out the shirt he was to wear. Over the years the man had indeed grown in stature and the shirt was far too tight to tie up at the front. This particular gentleman had a saying to all things and being "its damn fine". With this thought in mind Bessie cut the shirt up the back and made holes in which she fed through short pieces of material to tie in bows to allow the shirt to fit at the front and make the man presentable.

On asking her brother in law what he thought he mimicked the deceased and said "its damn fine". On hearing this Bessie once again burst into fits of laughter and it was a miracle that the poor man ever made his funeral. Bessie knew that at these times respect and dignity were paramount, but all she could think of was the neatly tied bows which donned the mans back where no-one was to see, what a damn fine job she had done of getting him ready.

Chapter 6

Leaving Stroma

Stroma Harbour

Although Stroma had a close community, with strong relationships, families started to leave the island. The island had gone from having a stronghold of 300 of a population in 1914 to approximately 108 when Bessie moved over to take up her position as district nurse and by 1957 there were only 45 people left.

With the provision of a new harbour costing around £30,000 pounds it seemed incredible that the time had finally come for people to leave and that the harbour had come too late. All the effort and determination of a community fighting for its rightful service of an adequate harbour facility seemed fruitless. Whether this was due to an ageing population, or whether the younger folk saw better opportunities on the mainland of Scotland, Bessie wasn't sure. Life was getting harder, and this had a knock-on effect for a lot of the older residents.

The local Co-operative Wholesale Society closed in 1956 and following that the Post Office finally closed in 1958, so provisions had to be ordered weekly to come from the mainland. Gradually everything started to get less and less. The schoolteacher had gone and, since Bessie's oldest son was supposed to start school in the autumn, they had to consider their options. The decision was inevitable and not taken lightly, but it was a sad day when Bessie, Sinclair and their family had to finally leave Stroma.

The Laird of Stroma had to pay the homeowners compensation for their houses and the sum of £125 for Sinclair's fathers house was paid, which was a lot of money in 1957. The majority of them accepted the compensation, although some people retained ownership of their island homes. I suppose it was somewhere they felt they could return to if they wanted to some day.

Some of the local crofters had shire-horses and, in one case, there was no way that the horse could be loaded on to a boat so, unfortunately, it had to be put down and buried on the island.

As Bessie and Sinclair prepared for their departure his brother-in-law came back across to Stroma to help with the move. Bessie can't remember taking many of their belongings although they must have had a few of their household items. It would have been impossible to take everything; therefore they only took the necessities. Everything was left in the nurse's cottage, both what had been there when they arrived, and also what they had added since, Bessie would have no use for a three legged table with her increasing family size.

Sinclair's father owned an organ, which had two push steps and was a big contraption, however it had been well looked after as the dark wood gleamed and was used regularly. It was despatched to the boat and taken over the Pentland Firth to take pride of place in their new home.

Unfortunately the Jeep had to be left on the island and as she looked at it for the last time Bessie remembered the times she had sped around the island in it. Sinclair sold it some time later for the same amount that he had originally paid for it so that helped a bit.

As the young couple looked around the island, they remembered the previous happy years spent on the island. As they scanned the horizon they saw the nurses cottage which had been their new home when they married. The school to the left untouched as the children had left it with books still sitting neatly where they had been set. The loch where many model sailing ships had set sail and competed was as still as a millpond and glistened from the sun.

As Bessie turned towards the Haven she looked at all the empty houses which had been inhabited by the couples she had visited on her rounds daily. Everything seemed so unreal and Bessie felt that she must have been dreaming, but it was reality and her and Sinclair had to face a different future for their family.

Bessie bundled the three bairns into the boat, followed by Sinclair and his father, and they set sail across the Pentland Firth to take up their new residence. It was a very sad day indeed as this had been Sinclair's home since birth and would be difficult to not only move to a strange house but find another way of supporting his family. What would it be like living somewhere else? He had never had to consider this as an option for the only time he had been away from home was when he was at the Wick High School and in the Navy but he had always been able to come home.

The Haven Stroma

As the boat made more distance from Stroma the island seemed insignificant in stature the further they sailed towards Huna. Bessie and Sinclair had their family and that was the important thing now and although the future was unknown they would start a new life together.

Bessie and Sinclair moved into a small but and ben called Sunbeam cottage, inside the old manse at Huna, it belonged to the church and was to be Bessie and Sinclair's home for eight weeks.

Not long after arriving on the mainland Sinclair eventually went and sat his formal driving test, however, before the test one of the requirements was to read a car number plate. Sinclair was having trouble seeing it, so he went and got a pair of glasses just for the test.

Bessie wasn't sure if Sinclair's glasses had helped him pass his test first time, or whether it was because it was Harvest Thanksgiving and the streets of Wick were nearly empty, allowing him the free run of the streets. She will never know but whatever way, Sinclair never wore the glasses again. He came home with a driving licence, and bought a Ford Anglia car to be their new transport. Bessie, not having a formal licence, despite driving in her jeep on Stroma was unable to drive on the mainland.

Sinclair originally wanted to work in the wireless office, as he had trained as radio officer in the merchant navy, and enjoyed it immensely, but at that time jobs were for life and very few folk left before they retired, allowing any new career opportunities. At that time he didn't have a hope of getting the job he wanted, so, when he had the opportunity to join the coastguard service instead he took the job, and ended up working at Wick Coastguard Station.

Along with the job, Sinclair was provided with a house which wasn't furnished, but they did have an organ and a few bits and pieces to start furnishing it. Bessie and Sinclair attended the local auction mart to buy some additional necessities for they had three children and Sinclair's father to accommodate. The coastguard station was situated just a mile outside Wick, seventeen miles east of Groats, and there was enough room for Sinclair and Bessie, his father and the bairns.

This was where Bessie and Sinclair began their new life and further enlarged their family to seven, but that's another story.

Lightning Source UK Ltd.
Milton Keynes UK
02 December 2009

146974UK00002BA/15/P